FROM
DILEMMA
TO
DELIGHT

CREATIVE IDEAS FOR HAPPY SABBATHS

D1005192

FROM
DILEMMA
TO
DELIGHT

CREATIVE IDEAS FOR HAPPY SABBATHS

GERITA GARVER LIEBELT

REVIEW AND HERALD PUBLISHING ASSOCIATION
Washington, DC 20039-0555
Hagerstown, MD 21740

Copyright © 1986 by
Review and Herald Publishing Association

This book was
Edited by Richard W. Coffen
Designed by Richard Steadham
Cover photo by Meylan Thoresen
Type set: 11/12 Bookman

PRINTED IN U.S.A.

Library of Congress Cataloging in Publication Data

Liebelt, Gerita Garver, 1950-
 From dilemma to delight.

 1. Sabbath. 2. Family—Religious life. 3. Seventh-
day Adventists—Doctrines. I. Title.
BX6154.L525   1986   263'.1   85-24433
ISBN 0-8280-0298-3

In Appreciation

I wish to thank Sandy Peterson and Eileen Lantry for planting the seeds that have flourished and grown within my heart for the past several years. Chiefly because of these women do I have an experience to tell! I am indebted to them for nearly all of the nature activity ideas I've used, although I adapted and changed them to fit my own family's needs.

I am also grateful to Ann Clark and Ellen Melore for the many helpful suggestions they made.

Many of my ideas are not new or original with me, but it's the story of my personal experience that I wish to share, hoping to encourage anyone else who might become discouraged like I was.

Many thanks also to my dear family for their patience and encouragement.

May God add His blessing is my prayer.

Contents

How It All Began

"If you keep your feet from breaking the Sabbath and from doing as you please on my holy day, if you call the Sabbath a delight . . ." (Isa. 58:13, N.I.V.).

The Sabbath a *delight? Delight* is such a pleasant-sounding word. I think of some of the things that I find delightful: a spectacular sunrise; the feeling of strength in my husband's embrace; a cuddlesome toddler; fresh brown, crusty bread; a leisurely bath at the end of a busy day; clean sheets sun-dried in the wind; the thick aroma of gardenias; warm, sunny days.

But I'm afraid that for a long time I would not have readily included the Sabbath on my list of delightful things. As a young minister's wife and mother of small children, I found that the days of the week seemed to run and blend together in one ceaseless round of activity. Sabbath for us is one of the busiest days of the week. And, of course, it always follows Friday, the most exhausting day of all. Unconsciously I would heave a little sigh of relief when these two busy days were over.

9

It was one autumn in Wyoming when the days were getting crisper *and* shorter. I can vividly remember a particular Friday a couple of months after our baby son was born. It had been an extremely busy day, and the sun was fast disappearing behind those Big Horn Mountains. The telephone kept stealing precious moments, and I knew that if my husband had any shirt at all to preach in the next day, I must somehow move the ironing board to within the radius of the telephone cord! Finally I literally jumped into the bathtub and sprayed warm water over my face. I distinctly remember the overwhelming desire to stay right there and soak for hours! Every muscle cried out to relax, but no, the sun was setting. Time for sundown worship and then a brief night's rest. The Sabbath a *delight?*

Sabbath mornings always meant a race to get the children and myself ready for church, beds made, pets fed, and the table cleared in half the time it usually required for such things. (And children never seem to be in a hurry!) Next came my Sabbath school duties, usually leading out in one of the divisions, and then the opportunity for me to stretch my mind to the very limit of its creativity to keep our little children quiet and still through the sermon—with no daddy available to help. The mere fact that everyone was watching to see how the minister's children behaved only added to my stress.

Then there might be company for dinner. I never knew exactly how many or who. I was just supposed to be prepared. Learning to cook healthfully was great, but my inexperience left me nervous and wondering how our varied guests would accept our meals. Afterward I had to face the piles of dirty white china in both kitchen sinks and an afternoon of trying to keep tabs on the children while at the same time trying to keep up a semblance of conversation with our guests. I found it impossible to do both things very well. By evening all I really wanted was someone to help put the children to bed so I could sink into mine. A delight? Not really!

The years went by, and at times I caught myself feeling rebellious—to a greater or lesser degree, of course, depending on the behavior of the children in church, the success of the meal, or the extent of exhaustion my body had reached. I felt perplexed because in the back of my mind I knew that if time should last I might have to give my life in favor of this day called Sabbath. But how could I ever do so when it was not the special kind of day that I felt the Lord had in mind for it to be? Sabbaths certainly were not the little oases of refreshment that I so desperately needed in my busy life. More often than not they were the unsatisfying climax to every week.

Then one bright normal day our refrigerator broke down! Dallas Peterson came to repair it, and his wife, Sandy, came too. Brown-eyed and soft-spoken, she came loaded down with her education materials that I was interested in. All of a sudden, deep within her resource material,

11

my eyes caught something. I felt like reaching out and grabbing it as a starving man would reach out to a table loaded with delicious food. Sandy had collected some 5 x 7 index cards; four of them were entitled "Preparing for the Sabbath," and twenty-eight were headed "Sabbath Activities." I devoured them hungrily and immediately wanted to share my discoveries with everyone!

"O taste and see that the Lord is good" the Bible says (Ps. 34:8), and I was tasting! Of course, when I offered my new findings to my children, they tasted and were delighted! In fact, one rainy Sabbath a few weeks later, our little 5-year-old said, "This is the best Sabbath we've ever had!" But the Lord was only preparing me for more. At camp meeting a few months later, one of the speakers casually mentioned a book that she had enjoyed. My ears pricked up at the title, *A Family Guide to Sabbath Nature Activities,* by Eileen E. Lantry.

I immediately headed for the campground bookstore, but her book was all sold out! Several months later I was able to get a copy and was thrilled beyond measure. I found that the Sabbath can be a delight! And as I searched, with heart yearning, for meaning to the Sabbath, the rest of Isaiah 58:13, 14 came true in my life. "If you call the Sabbath a delight and the Lord's holy day honorable, and if you honor it by not going your own way and not doing as you please or speaking idle words, *then you will find your joy in the Lord"* (N.I.V.). Each Sabbath gets better than the one before as I learn a little bit more about the true purpose and beauty of this very special day.

A Rainbow
of Answers

"I do set my bow in the cloud, and it shall be for a token of a covenant between me and the earth" (Gen. 9:13).

Growing up with the Sabbath truth, I had readily accepted it and never rejected it, but somehow in the rush of life with the added responsibilities of a family, the Sabbath became more of a ritual than something deeply appreciated and treasured. I wasn't comfortable with my feelings, so I determined to search for some answers.

As I began to study the Sabbath with a newly awakened interest it seemed that each Bible truth was like a brilliant band of color that flashed across my mind with fresh meaning. Each new discovery was like another band of color that blended with the others until a rainbow of colors brought light and beauty to my soul. Let me share with you some of the discoveries that I found exciting.

Number one. God Himself keeps the Sabbath. In Genesis 2:2, 3 we see that a tireless God stopped to rest on the seventh day, then gave it a special blessing and set it apart for holy use. How does this relate to me? It seems that God never asks us to do anything that He does not do Himself! He is not like a parent who lords it over us, saying, "Do as I say and not as I do." I like that.

Number two. Even Adam and Eve, in a perfect world, needed the Sabbath. "God reserved the seventh day as a period of rest for man, for the good of man as well as for His own glory. He saw that the wants of man required a day of rest from toil and care, that his health and life would be endangered without a period of relaxation from the labor and anxiety of the six days. The Sabbath was made for the benefit of man."—*Testimonies,* vol. 1, pp. 532, 533.

How does this relate to me? All the "restrictions" of the Sabbath are for my *benefit!* And *properly observed,* the Sabbath brings total health and refreshment to body, soul, and mind. I really like that!

Number three. The Sabbath was very important in Old Testament times. God placed the Sabbath command in the very center of the Decalogue. The children of Israel, God's chosen missionaries to the world, had their ups and downs, however, and would often grow slack in their observance of the Sabbath. Jeremiah, Nehemiah, and Ezekiel strongly denounced Sabbathbreaking and pleaded for revival (see Jeremiah 17, Nehemiah 13, and Ezekiel 20). It was the polluting of the Sabbath that kept the

15

Exodus Israelites out of the Promised Land (Eze. 20:15, 16), and eventually brought about the destruction of Jerusalem (see Jer. 17:27).

They certainly were slow to learn, we might think. But all these things were written as examples for us. Is my life one of spiritual ups and downs, and will I miss the Promised Land for the same reason?

Number four. The Sabbath is *the sign* between God's people and Him. "And hallow my sabbaths; and they shall be a sign between me and you, that ye may know that I am the Lord your God" (Eze. 20:20). I had known this truth most of my life, but it was my next discovery about this sign that really thrilled me.

The marriage relationship is one of the ways the Bible illustrates the relationship between God and His people. "For thy Maker is thine husband; the Lord of hosts is his name; and thy Redeemer the Holy One of Israel; The God of the whole earth shall he be called" (Isa. 54:5). "And I will betroth thee unto me for ever; yea, I will betroth thee unto me in righteousness, and in judgment, and in lovingkindness, and in mercies" (Hosea 2:19). Paul spoke to the New Testament Christians about his role as a minister in this relationship: "For I am jealous over you with godly jealousy: for I have espoused you to one husband, that I may present you as a chaste virgin to Christ" (2 Cor. 11:2).

This marriage relationship with Christ is the only way we can take Christ's name and go home and live with Him for eternity. The Sabbath, God's seal, is like the marriage certificate—the seal proves we are His and He is ours.

How Satan has worked to pervert the marriage relationship in our day so that the full significance of this symbol is not appreciated or understood! Nevertheless, we must take Christ's name (and bear it proudly), become one with Him (in our thoughts and desires), have the spirit of love (it prevents a legalistic relationship), and remain faithful "till death do us part."

How does this relate to me? I found that I couldn't have just a weekend relationship with God. I had expected my Sabbath blessings to come automatically at sundown Friday night and for some reason fade with the glow of the setting sun Saturday night. I discovered, then, that true Sabbathkeeping does not begin Friday night and end Sabbath evening at sundown. If we have truly fallen in love with our Saviour (and that should happen before marriage—baptism—but sometimes it happens after) we have a vital connection with Him that fills every moment. All week long our thoughts turn to the One we love! I discovered that the closer I stayed to the Lord all week, the more special Sabbath was for me at the end of the week. We busy mothers must take the time to meet daily with our Maker, or our love for Him will become merely a ritual, and every restriction a burden. A marriage cannot flourish without communication.

Number five. The three final messages given

from Heaven to our perishing world before the second coming of Christ urge us to keep the Sabbath and our marriage covenant with Jesus. We refer to these messages as the three angels' messages of Revelation 14. I knew they held significance to our church but never fully understood why. I was excited as I saw how beautifully they all fit together, carrying out the theme of the entire Bible.

The first angel's message is "Fear God, and give glory to him for the hour of his judgment is come . . ' . ". (verse 7). This judgment is an investigative judgment in which heaven's books are opened (Dan. 7:9, 10). It is also referred to as the cleansing of the sanctuary, which, we can figure from the time prophecy of Daniel 8:14, began in October of 1844 and is still going on in heaven. Before Christ comes, a decision must be made as to who is united with Him and who is eligible to feast at the marriage supper of the Lamb, because it is after the wedding that Christ comes (see Luke 12:36, 37). The pronouncement of eligibility, or judgment, is the final thing Christ does just before He returns (see Rev. 14:14). We are to enter the wedding *now* with Christ, by faith, for soon the wedding will be over, and then it will be forever too late!

We are living during the time when the bride is to make herself ready—the time when the sanctuary is to be cleansed. "Let us be glad and rejoice, and give honour to him: for the marriage of the Lamb is come, and his wife hath made herself ready. And to her was granted that she should be arrayed in fine linen, clean and white: for the fine linen is the righteousness of saints" (chap. 19:7, 8). "Husbands, love your wives, even as Christ also loved the church, and gave himself for it; that he might sanctify and cleanse it with the washing of water by the word, that he might present it to himself a glorious church, not having spot, or wrinkle, or any such thing; but that it should be holy and without blemish" (Eph. 5:25-27).

This awesome work involves the last part of the *first* angel's message: "And worship him that made heaven, and earth, and the sea, and the fountains of waters." Do you hear the echo of the fourth commandment? The Sabbath commandment is the one that tells us to worship the Creator of "heaven and earth, the sea, and all that in them is" (Ex. 20:11).

"The time for the commandments of God to shine out with all their importance, and for God's people to be tried on the Sabbath truth, was when the door was opened in the most holy place in the heavenly sanctuary, where the ark is, in which are contained the ten commandments. This door was not opened until the mediation of Jesus was finished in the holy place of the sanctuary in 1844. Then Jesus rose up and shut the door of the holy place, and opened the door into the most holy, and passed within the second veil, where He now stands by the ark, and where the faith of Israel now reaches.

"I say that Jesus had shut the door of the holy place, and no man can open it; and that He had opened the door into the most holy, and no man can shut it (Rev. 3:7, 8); and that since Jesus has opened the door into the most holy place, which contains the ark, the commandments have been shining out to God's people, and they are being tested on the Sabbath question."—*Early Writings,* p. 42.

The second angel's message is "Babylon is fallen, is fallen, that great city, because she made all nations drink of the wine of the wrath of her fornication" (chap. 14:8). "Come out of her, my people, that ye be not partakers of her sins, and that ye receive not of her plagues" (chap. 18:4). We see the marriage relationship used again here. Churches are Biblically represented by women, either pure and faithful or impure and unfaithful (see Ephesians 5 and Revelation 17). Babylon is the church of spiritual whoredom. She does not obey Christ, her head and husband. She has fallen away from His leading. This second angel's message is for God's people to separate themselves from the whore and unite themselves in a pure and undefiled way with Christ. And the Sabbath is the marriage certificate that proves we are His and He is ours.

The third angel's message is "If any man worship the beast and his image, and receive his mark in his forehead, or in his hand, the same shall drink of the wine of the wrath of God, which is poured out without mixture into the cup of his indignation; and he shall be tormented with fire and brimstone in the presence of the holy angels, and in the presence of the Lamb: and the smoke of their torment ascendeth up for ever and ever: and they have no rest day nor night, who worship the beast and his image, and whosoever receiveth the mark of his name" (Rev. 14:9-11). Here the revelator portrays the eternal doom of those who have the mark of the beast. In contrast, the saints *"keep the commandments of God"* (verse 12). God has a mark too, and His mark is the loyal keeping of His Sabbath day. God says this is His "sign between me and you, that ye may know that I am the Lord your God" (Eze. 20:20).

Right before the Second Coming there will be only two groups of people on the face of the earth: those who are married to Christ and those who are not. And the Sabbath is like the marriage certificate, God's sanctifying seal that proves we are His and He is ours. Most Christians regard nine of the ten commandments as binding in their relationship with God and man. But many have set aside and forgotten the fourth commandment. Ironically, it's the only commandment that begins with the word *remember!*

How does this relate to me? I myself must remain loyally united with Christ, and then, as He has asked me, help remind the world to "remember." And there's not much time left in which to do so! But how does a person actually *remember* the Sabbath day to keep it *holy?*

How to Remember

"Choose you this day whom ye will serve" (Joshua 24:15).

I can remember a time in college when my husband-to-be and I were courting. He had to take a trip that lasted for several days. I looked forward so eagerly for the night of his return! I fairly flew down the dormitory stairs when I was paged. You do that when you're in love, you know! We visited until the very last possible moment. Even then we lingered—just wanting to be close to each other!

On the other hand, can you picture me launching into some big project the day of his return (such as repainting the room) and working myself to a frazzle up to the very minute of his arrival? What if I had never bothered to change my work clothes or fix my hair? What if I came down late to the lobby after being paged to greet him? What if I had been so tired I couldn't keep back my yawns, and finally excused myself early "to get some rest"? Unthinkable! And he would have wondered how important he really was to me. He might even have wondered whether I had chosen someone else to center my affections on.

I think God must often feel this way. He eagerly looks forward to our special time together each Sabbath. The God of the universe, the mighty Creator of worlds and space, seeks after us. He tenderly guards communication time with us, knowing that such time together is vital to our relationship. Doesn't it make your heart skip a beat to realize He's such a thoughtful, considerate God? O how He must love us! From the beginning He has chosen us (2 Thess. 2:13). But have we chosen *Him?* Do we look forward enough to this special time with Him each week to plan our clothes, tidy our home, and groom our hair? Or do we allow ourselves to work so hard that we collapse as soon as Sabbath comes?

"None should permit themselves, through the week, to become so absorbed in their temporal interests, and so exhausted by their efforts for worldly gain, that on the Sabbath they have no strength or energy to give to the service of God. We are robbing the Lord when we unfit ourselves to worship Him upon His holy day."—*Child Guidance,* p. 530.

Perhaps we should rethink some of our priorities in light of the wise counsel given in Psalm 127:2: "It is senseless for you to work so hard from early morning until late at night, fearing you will starve to death; for God wants his loved ones to get their proper rest" (T.L.B.). God must have put that verse there especially for our working generation of today!

Yes, remembering the Sabbath involves

choosing whom we really love. It also involves choosing which activities are really priorities *every morning of the week.* During this time of my life while my children are small, mothering requires most of my time and energy. I must drastically streamline my optional activities. I may have to skip a Tupperware party or shopping trip because I want to be fresh, relaxed, and happy when Sabbath comes. And I can't be that way if I take on too many extra projects during the week.

It was canning season, and I was filling cupboards as fast as I could with jars of tomatoes, plums, and applesauce. In addition, one of the ladies in our church had promised to give me her Concord grapes when they ripened. Free! She finally called on a Thursday and said that the grapes needed to be picked right away! There was no way that my husband or I could pick them and juice them that Thursday. I was toying with the idea of going over and picking them Friday morning when she continued, "Even if you do get them all done Friday by working hard, you'll enter the Sabbath hours so tired." I thought to myself, She's right! Even if the grapes don't keep till Sunday, my time with my Saviour is worth more than all the grape juice in the world. So I waited—and the grapes did keep. I've found that putting the Lord first is never a bad choice. Each day we must choose whom we will serve.

Another look at the fourth commandment

tells us how to remember the Sabbath day: "Six
days shalt thou labour, and do all thy work . . . "
Washing, ironing, mending, cookig, and cleaning all must be done before sundown Friday
night. Even our baths should be taken so that we
will be fresh and clean for God.

But we have *six* days each week until the
Sabbath comes, and each day should count in
preparation for it. I used to leave all my getting-
ready work until Friday. After all, that was the
preparation day, wasn't it? But invariably Friday
would be the day that company would come or
the electricity would go off or the basement would
flood!

I'll never forget how embarrassed I was one
Sabbath. Our church had just conducted Vacation Bible School that week, and of course, our
whole family had been involved. Being away from
home every day for about five hours didn't leave
much time for the home chores. Each day I kept
putting off getting my Sabbath preparation
done. By Friday afternoon I barely had time to
dash home, prepare two blackberry cobblers (one
for our breakfast and one for a family in our
church), fix some potatoes for Sabbath dinner,
give the children their baths and wash their hair,
iron our Sabbath clothes, and dash back to the
church for the closing program of Vacation Bible
School.

"The house will just have to wait this week," I
whispered to myself as I slid into a pew. "Anyway,
we're not having company."

Then Sabbath morning some new friends of ours drove quite a distance and showed up unexpectedly in church. Of course, I had to invite them home for dinner. I very clearly remember jumping out of our car before it even came to a full stop in our carport, running into the house, and heading straight for the bathrooms. "Try to talk to them awhile outside before you bring them in," I implored my husband. And I quickly threw things into drawers, wiped out the sinks, and washed the spatters off the mirrors.

That evening I had a little talk with myself. For whom was I cleaning my house? Did I just clean my house on Fridays for the Sabbath guests that might come? Or did I clean my house every Friday in anticipation of meeting with God?

I heard of a church member who thought she had the nicest neighbor. In fact, one Sabbath as she sat in church she saw some visitors whom she felt she must invite home for dinner. Quickly she got up, phoned her neighbor, and asked her to run over to her house and straighten it up for her. The neighbor was truly a wonderful lady. She promptly went over and, as I remember, made the beds, washed the dishes, and picked up for her Adventist neighbor. On two different Sabbaths this happened. And both times the Adventist woman invited the visitors over for dinner, it turned out they already had dinner plans!

But what kind of witness was this to the non-Adventist neighbor? What about that part of the Sabbath command that says, "Thou shalt not do any work, thou . . . nor thy stranger that is within thy gates"? Why not prepare our homes ahead of time each week in honor of our Creator, who sees all things?

I finally figured out a weekly schedule that works wonders for me. It's really quite simple and adaptable. By doing one thing each day of the week in preparation for Sabbath, I can be prepared at the end of the week without feeling too hurried. For example: Monday I wash the Sabbath clothes; Tuesday I iron them; Wednesday I plan the Sabbath menu and the Sabbath day's activities and do the shopping; Thursday I bake and prepare food for the Sabbath meals. That leaves Friday, when I complete the preparation. I've found that with small children I must wait until Friday to do the housecleaning, or by Friday night I'd never know it had been done!

I was surprised a few years ago when I overheard both my older children say emphatically, "I hate Fridays!" I could sense the conclusion to their thinking: "It's because of Sabbath that we have to work so hard on Fridays!" That was the way I had previously felt, and I didn't want them feeling the same way. I gave it some serious thought and reminded myself that children don't like to be rushed! (Who does?) I have found that if I faithfully do my Sabbath preparation all through the week, it takes a lot of the rush and hurry out of my voice on Fridays. After all, there's enough stress in our environment without making Friday such a stressful day!

So I decided to explain to the children the purpose of preparing to keep the Sabbath, according to the commandment. I also determined to make the preparation as much fun as possible. So at breakfasttime on Friday mornings I would get out slips of paper and write out a list of things for everyone to do for the day. Of course, our little children couldn't read, so I'd sketch a picture of each thing on their list, and when they'd complete a job they could mark it off just like Mom! Following are some of the things I've found that little people can do very well and enjoy doing.

If you have clothes to fold, the children can help by sorting them into piles: all their clothes in one pile, all Mommy's clothes in a pile, all Daddy's in another pile, all towels and washcloths in another pile, et cetera. Or they can pretend that the socks are twins that belong to a large family. After they find all the twins, Mom can roll them up. Then the children can "tuck the socks into bed" in the respective dresser drawers.

Children can gather all the wastebaskets throughout the house and set them by the door to be taken out. This can be a "gold rush," all the trash being gold to search for and dig out!

Children can straighten the shoes in all the closets. Each closet can be a "room" in "Noah's ark," and each animal (each shoe) needs to stand beside its mate, two by two, before the Flood

28

(sundown) comes.

Make a "train" out of the dining room chairs that need dusting. Now is the time to teach your youngsters the correct way to dust. It may seem a little time-consuming or expensive at first (when you see their liberal use of the furniture polish, for instance), but don't give up. Someday you will be well repaid by their willingness to share in lifting the family burdens.

Doing dishes can be fun for a child who's old enough to dry them. We've played lots of games with this chore. Sometimes the dishes are "vegetables" that we are planting in the garden (dishwater). The rains come (the rinsing), and then they're harvested (dried) and put into our cupboards for "winter." Plates can be heads of cabbage or cauliflower. Knives can be stalks of celery, and the forks can be carrots. Spoons can be green beans—or whatever your imagination comes up with. Or you can have a birthday party, and all the dishes are the "people" you invite. The big dishes represent the adults, and the spoons are the babies.

Everyday books and magazines can be put out of sight or in bookcases according to the counsel in *Child Guidance*, page 528: "Before the setting of the sun, let all secular work be laid aside, and all secular papers be put out of sight."

At our house it has really helped to have the children lay out their own Sabbath clothes on Friday. Then there's no last-minute misunderstanding as to what they will wear, there are no missing belts, *both* shoes are present and cleaned, and the children can dress quietly and without confusion on Sabbath morning.

As the hours of the Sabbath draw near I try to avoid anything that might cause my children to enter the sacred hours in an unhappy frame of mind. I have assigned any unpleasant jobs earlier in the day. And when bath time comes perhaps you could let the children use bubble bath (just on Friday afternoons) as a special get-ready-for-the-Sabbath treat.

Now to set the mood for worship. I enjoy playing beautiful religious songs an hour *before* sunset so that the music can help turn everyone's thoughts heavenward. When I hear the name Tennessee Ernie Ford, it brings memories of my Texas home, of the smell of furniture polish, and of a golden living room as the sun shone in on Friday afternoons. As a young girl I pondered over one song he used to sing, "Others," and how even our prayers should be for others. That was an entirely new thought to my young mind. Even today, flashes of that song come to me and inspire me to be more unselfish. We as parents should use good music to our advantage in the training of our children. It's a priceless gift from God. The right kind of music seems to put a melody in our hearts and harmony in our home.

We've talked about home preparation for Sabbath. Did you know that there's to be heart preparation also? "There is another work that should receive attention on the preparation day. On this day all differences between brethren, whether in the family or in the church, should be put away."—*Ibid.*, pp. 528, 529).

I have found myself needing to say some things similar to "Honey, I'm sorry I snapped back at you during dinner today when you mentioned the burnt potatoes." Or "Children, forgive me for being impatient with you this afternoon."

What a sweet feeling of peace there is when we've asked forgiveness and been forgiven and our hearts are ready for the blessings of heaven!

To Remember
First comes choosing,
Then comes preparing,
Then comes savoring
Our Sabbath rest!

Friday
Night

"O come, let us worship and bow down: let us kneel before the Lord our maker" (Ps. 95:6).

What a privilege it is to worship! To worship means to love or to honor with intense devotion. When we worship God we bring honor and glory to Him. How can we help our children worship Him? Teaching and instructing them about God is one way to inspire reverence and love for Him. They also need to be able to enter into the worship service and become actively involved for themselves.

Ideally, worship should begin *before* the setting of the sun on Friday evening. And Friday night worships should be special because the Sabbath is special. Here are a few ideas that I've found make happy Friday nights with the family while we worship God together.

When the days are short, a candlelight service is a nice way to begin the Sabbath. One year for our vacation our family stayed for two weeks in an isolated log cabin in the green, green mountains of Idaho. There was no running water or electricity, of course, and so in the dark of the evenings with the shadows of the stately ever-greens pressing in around us, we would light the candles. Lots of them! Then while the wood stove crackled we would read portions of *The Great Controversy*—stories of the brave and faithful Waldenses and of the grand and dramatic scenes at the end of time. Somehow, in the flickering candlelight, our imaginations could grasp the importance and reality of these past and future events.

There's something special about candlelight. If they're old enough, let your children light the candles. Or for an object lesson, begin with the room totally dark. Then light a candle and say, "Jesus is the light of the world." Sing songs about letting our lights shine, and talk about how we can do this or about the ways a person might hide his light.

For the long summer evenings, have worship outdoors. One Friday evening my husband and I told the children we were going to pretend we were a part of Abraham's family and worship just as they did long ago. We all walked down the lane from our house to a little clearing. There we stopped and began hunting for stones with which to build an altar. After the children and their father built the altar and put sticks on top, there were questioning looks that said, What now? We talked about the lamb for the offering, and then from my pocket I took a white card that had the letters J E S U S printed on it and laid it on the altar. We sat on the ground and talked about the wonderful sacrifice of Jesus.

These outdoor worships are ideal times for a testimony-and-praise or thank-you-thoughts service. Or have poem night, when each member of the family brings a poem to read. Children love poetry. In fact, our three children enjoy making up their own poems. One worship we made up a poem about the Sabbath school lesson for that week. Each of us thought of a stanza, and then we put them all together. Here's what we came up with in just a few minutes. Can you guess what our lesson was about that week?

> David couldn't build the church,
> But all the materials he could search.
> The church was built upon the ground,
> And it was built without a sound.
> The Temple was filled with a great pink
>   cloud.
> In church we never should be loud.
> Solomon prayed a prayer so long—
> Then all the people sang a song!

Our family also enjoys acting out the children's Sabbath school lesson. For instance, one time their lesson was on the resurrection of Jesus. We draped a brown sleeping bag over the end of the dining room table, making a "tomb." Our boy, Michael, wrapped a sheet around himself and lay under the table. Our girl, Tracey, wrapped a sheet around herself and played the part of Gabriel. Our toddler, Mindy, and I made two fine soldiers with our stick spears. Every lesson has the potential to come alive and be meaningful if done reverently.

If you have felts, you might want to save them for Friday night worships, letting one of the children tell the story on the felt board to the rest of the family.

On another Friday night ask everyone to draw or color a picture of something he remembers in the Sabbath school lesson. The children's lesson for one particular week was about the Lord's Supper. Our 5-year-old boy thought awhile and then drew twelve cups with his ink marker. That's all. His older sister's drawing was, of course, more elaborate. By the way, some of these pictures can turn out to be a mother's valuable keepsakes!

Primary-age children enjoy listening to tapes. If you're so fortunate as to have "The Bible in Living Sound," find the tape with the week's Bible lesson on it and listen to it for worship.

Another idea would be to get a set of Bible study filmstrips, such as the Encounter set, which is very interesting and easy to understand. If this is impossible, borrow some filmstrips from your church or pastor and have a Bible study each Friday night, going through the great doctrines of our faith. A Dukane projector or similar machine works beautifully, and many churches have access to one for the members to use in their witnessing.

It's always nice to have special stories just for

Friday night—perhaps a continued one or stories of missionaries and other great pioneers for God. Have some special Bible games just for Friday night, too. Our family enjoys The Ungame, which is available at any Christian bookstore.

Occasionally you might want to invite another family to come and present a special worship for your children. An older couple or single adult would probably love to do this for you. I knew of a family in our area that had the sanctuary felt set. I was interested in teaching this subject to our children but couldn't afford to buy the felt set. So I invited them to come over for a Friday evening worship and present this topic to us.

A special Friday night treat for small children is for the girls to have the privilege of sleeping with Mother and the boys with Father—at least until the children fall asleep. Our youngsters really look forward to this privilege. And without fail the topic for discussion after we're in bed is heaven! We enjoy letting our imaginations run wild with this delightful subject. For example, we like to guess what God's welcome-home menu will be, what special things Jesus will have for the children to do, what God's throne will look like, and how interesting the books will be in heaven's library! We try to get an early start so that our fun talks won't go on past the usual bedtime hour. If you want to enjoy some wonderful descriptions of heaven, read *Early Writ-*

ings, pages 13-20, and *The Adventist Home*, pages 542, 543, 546-549.

For older children, a regular Friday night back rub at bedtime might be appreciated. It's a marvelous opportunity to get close to my children and speak to them about the direction of their lives and the matchless charms of Jesus. It's also one of the best ways I've found to check rebellion and to close the generation gap. It helps keep me in tune with my children's needs, fears, and joys, and it lets me guide them to the Source of all solutions.

Whatever you choose to do to make Friday night special—do it regularly so that the children can count on it and look forward to it. These are the times that build memories and bind the hearts of our little ones to us and to our Creator.

Worship is over. The children are asleep, and the house is still. I pause to thank the Lord for these first few Sabbath hours. They've been delightful. I also thank Him for His presence, which has put the feeling of love and peace in our home. I can hardly wait for morning to come!

Sabbath Morning

"God is spirit, and those who worship him must worship in spirit and truth" (John 4:24).

When I finally connected the meaning of this verse to the Sabbath, it was as if the pieces of a puzzle fell into place. The seventh-day Sabbath is clearly truth, but we must have the *spirit* of the Sabbath if we are to keep it holy.

Remember, in a marriage two people can be legally united, but unless they have a spirit of love for each other, the union is not complete. We are to be one with Christ. He wants us to keep the Sabbath holy mentally and spiritually as well as physically.

I found that the spirit of Sabbathkeeping is that of joyful and holy celebration. God said, "From even unto even, shall ye celebrate your sabbath" (Lev. 23:22). This particular verse refers to the Day of Atonement, but I feel that the principle is the same for each weekly Sabbath. The word *celebrate* refers to a joyous occasion. Isaiah 56:6, 7 tells us that God will make joyful those who keep the Sabbath and don't pollute it.

For children, this spirit seems to be caught more than taught. It sort of rubs off on them! No wonder Paul writes, "Rejoice in the Lord alway: and again I will say, Rejoice" (Phil. 4:14).

We are also told to keep the Sabbath holy by not doing *our own* ways, nor finding *our own* pleasure, nor speaking *our own* words (Isa. 58:13). This tells me we are to think of something other than ourselves for twenty-four hours. On the Sabbath every thought and every action should draw our minds away from self to our wonderful Creator.

We are so immersed in the sin and selfishness of this world, however, that it takes some thought and planning to keep our thoughts and the thoughts of our children selfless and heavenward for an entire day! First of all, I've found it essential to pray this prayer of David: "Create in me a clean heart, O God; and renew a right spirit within me" (Ps. 51:10). And in Ezekiel 36:26 God promises to do just that. Only God can create in us clean hearts and right spirits, because He is the Creator, which the Sabbath always reminds us of.

Here are some things that have helped our family celebrate the Sabbath and keep it in *spirit* and in *truth*.

As a rule our family has always had worship before breakfast. But somehow on rushed Sabbath mornings I would rationalize, "We don't have to have worship before breakfast on Sabbath because we'll be worshipping at church later on." My husband and I finally concluded that to keep the Sabbath holy we needed on this day, more than on any other, to start out huddled together as a family and asking for God's presence and blessing.

If a football team needs to huddle together often for encouragement and direction, should we as a family do less? A team does it for earthly glory; we do it to bring glory to God. Perhaps we'll no longer be able to sleep in on Sabbath mornings, but the unity of the family is well worth it.

I've also had to work hard on my constant commands to the children to hurry up! One Sabbath I determined not to say "Hurry up" even once. But before I knew it, I had said it! I quickly started to sing while I combed heads of hair so that I wouldn't slip again. Do you know, we were on time that morning, and everyone in the family seemed so much happier!

So on Sabbath mornings let the family rise early. Eliminate any hurrying or impatience. Sacred music can set a beautiful atmosphere for waking up everyone. And worship together—just as a family.

There are many ways to turn thoughts heavenward just by the way the table is set at breakfasttime. Remember, today is a joyful occasion! Use special place mats or tablecloths. (Make your own place mats and cover them with clear contact paper, if you wish.) Be creative with the way you fold the napkins or use candles. I find it helpful to set the table for breakfast the night before.

When possible I like to buy pretty paper bowls and matching plates that I won't have to wash. Sometimes I just use plain paper plates, and in the middle of each plate I write a Bible verse or love note to each member of the family. Then I cover the message with an upside-down cereal bowl for a special surprise.

When Tracey was a toddler she loved to put pretty stickers of animals or Bible characters in the middle of each bread plate. (They wash off easily.) Now that she's older and can read, I enjoy writing a Bible verse on each napkin and drawing a little picture to go with it. I use bright felt-tip pens. It's fun to choose an appropriate verse for each person, and it helps us all become better acquainted with the Bible.

For instance, if Daddy is going to sing for special music in church that day, Psalm 40:3 fits for him: "He hath put a new song in my mouth, even praise unto our God: many shall see it, and fear, and shall trust in the Lord." I draw a few musical notes around this verse on his napkin.

Or for the baby, Matthew 19:14 fits: "But Jesus said, Suffer little children, and forbid them not, to come unto me." I draw a picture of a baby.

Another verse for children might be Proverbs 25:11, which says: "A word fitly spoken is like apples of gold in pictures of silver." Apples are easy to draw.

If a particular child has been discouraged or troubled over something during the week, such as the death of a pet, Psalm 147:3 would be good: "He healeth the broken in heart, and bindeth up their wounds." Draw a picture of a heart.

The Bible has many texts applicable to every occasion, even to visitors and grandparents! If we have very many guests who are having breakfast with us, I resort to the speed of my typewriter. Surprisingly, the type comes out quite pretty on paper napkins, along with the bright felt-tip pictures.

In the summer I like to pick fresh flowers and place one beside each setting. The conversation can then center upon the question "Isn't God the most wonderful artist to paint the colors of each flower so beautifully?" Then while we eat we can compare and talk about the flowers. Did you know that flowers need the help of bees and other insects to bring pollen to them so they can produce their seeds? Did you know that around their nectar source yellow flowers have dark ultraviolet markings that attract the bees? Look at your flowers closely and help your children find the stigma, anthers, pollen tube, and ovule. Talk about how God will clothe us like the flowers of the field. Remind the children that Jesus has been called the Lily of the valley and the Rose of Sharon.

In the fall, pick a sheaf of flaming leaves and arrange one beside each place and say, "God made every leaf on every tree." Isn't that an awesome thought! Then during breakfast talk about the leaves of the tree of life (Rev. 22:2) or about some of the interesting leaves mentioned elsewhere in the Bible, such as in Psalm 1:3. Did you know that "there are life-giving properties in the balsam of the pine, in the fragrance of the cedar and the fir, and other trees also have properties that are health restoring" (*The Ministry of Healing*, p. 264)?

Sometimes I make little name cards out of bright-colored construction paper cut in rectangles and folded in half lengthwise. Beside each person's name I put a Bible thought or sticker. These can be saved and used again later.

Here's another idea for bright-colored rectangles made from construction paper. Collect things in nature such as yellow leaves, pieces of bark, small feathers, dried flowers, or anything else small enough to fit nicely on the rectangles of paper. Let your children hunt for these items during the week, and then let them choose which background color goes best with each item. For instance, ask, "Do these two green acorns look better on orange paper or brown?" Then let the children glue them on and put one card at each plate Sabbath morning. They love it!

Which reminds me, very soon your children will want to be in charge of decorating the table with spiritual and natural themes for Sabbath. Even our little toddler got excited on a walk one day when she found a beautiful leaf. "Let's save it for happy Sabbath to go on the table," she said.

Perhaps you would prefer to burn some incense during breakfast and talk about how our prayers rise as sweet-smelling incense to our heavenly Father. Our offerings, sanctified words, and songs of praise also rise as sweet incense.

Anything that makes the breakfast table special and that reminds us of our Creator can be used to draw the thoughts and conversation heavenward.

Now for breakfast itself! Contemporary research reveals the close relationship between the kinds of food eaten and human behavior. For instance, table sugar is a known source of quick energy. "Excessive sugar and lack of vitamin B complex and certain minerals result in the incomplete metabolism of sugar," causing nerve damage that can result in irritability.[1]

In the Iowa Breakfast Study, scientists learned that those who omit breakfast suffer from increased fatigue, irritability, slowed reaction time, and a ten o'clock slump. Schoolchildren show better attitudes and scholastic attainments when they eat a good breakfast.[2]

With much wisdom, then, the mother should prepare Sabbath morning breakfast. She does not want her little ones to be hyperactive during church. They are active enough as it is! She does not want them irritable or restless. So she will provide a good breakfast that will keep them comfortable until dinnertime, not just until ten o'clock. And she wants the minds of her family alert and receptive to the words from God spoken in the church service.

If schoolchildren show better scholastic attainments in day school when they eat a good breakfast, surely it is even more important for those attending Sabbath school to eat a good breakfast. The original diet of whole-grain foods, natural fruits, and delicious nuts will accomplish this very nicely. It's the white-flour cinnamon rolls and sugar-coated cereals that work against us.

Here are some foods that our family enjoys for Sabbath morning breakfast. They are quick and easy to prepare and make a wholesome start for the day.

CORNBREAD 'N' GRAVY

2 cups warm water	⅓ cup applesauce
2 Tbsp. honey	1 Tbsp. oil
1 Tbsp. yeast	1 cup whole-wheat
2 cups fresh cornmeal	flour
1 tsp. salt	1 cup white flour

Mix together the warm water, honey, and yeast. Let set until the yeast is dissolved. Mix in rest of ingredients and pour into an oiled pan. Let rise and then bake at 350°F. for 30 minutes or until golden brown. Cover with tinfoil or reheat on Sabbath morning (this prevents it from drying out). Serve covered with a thick country-style milk gravy.

BLUEBERRIES ON RICE

Cook your rice on Friday and put it in a baking dish to reheat on Sabbath morning. For the topping, mix 2 cups of apple juice and 4 tablespoons of cornstarch together and cook until thick. Add blueberries to the topping just before serving. For variety, use thickened pineapple juice with pineapple chunks and serve over brown rice. Add sliced bananas on top or mix in raisins for color.

BANANA SPLITS

Split a fresh banana lengthwise for each person. Use an ice-cream scoop to place three scoops of hot cooked millet on top of the banana. Have handy your three favorite toppings and some chopped nuts to sprinkle on top. Our favorite toppings are peach, grape, and pineapple.

Peach Topping: Blend canned or frozen peaches (drained) and heat.

Grape Topping: Heat 1 cup grape juice with 1 cup raisins until they are plump. Then blend well. Add 2 more cups grape juice and bring to a boil in a saucepan. Mix 3 tablespoons cornstarch with 3 tablespoons water until smooth and add to the grape mixture, stirring until thick.

Pineapple Topping: Thicken 1 cup pineapple juice with 3 tablespoons cornstarch and bring to a boil. Add 1 or 2 cups crushed pineapple (drained). Heat.[3]

How to Cook Millet: Millet is a very nutritious whole grain. It comes from the hand of the

Creator filled with calcium, protein, iron, phosphorous, potassium, and smaller amounts of other good things. It has a mild flavor and is sold in natural-food stores.

To cook this grain, combine 1 cup millet, 4 cups water, and 1 teaspoon salt in a saucepan and bring to a boil. Then steam it in the top of a double boiler for 1 hour. After 30 minutes, stir and check water level in bottom of double boiler. It may also be cooked directly over heat, in a way similar to brown rice, until it is soft and fluffy. To do this, bring to a boil, then simmer covered for 45 to 60 minutes. This can be cooked on Friday and put in a casserole dish to reheat in the oven Sabbath morning.[4]

Of course, we like cold cereals for a change, too. There are several good cereals out that are whole grain and contain no sugar.

With your cereal, try a rabbit salad made of a pear half, cut side down, for the body. Cut a peeled apple wedge in half for the ears, and add a small marshmallow or round banana slice for the puff of a tail. Seat him on a lettuce leaf or in a clump of alfalfa sprout "grass."

Or try four pear halves, cut side down, shaped like the four wings of a butterfly. Have an apple wedge body and antennae, and add nuts or raisins to the tops of the pears for designs appropriate to butterflies. Bread sticks might be enough to complement this fruit plate.

Now is a good time to talk about these delightful creatures at the breakfast table.

Explain how God protects them.

For a simple sunflower salad, peel and separate a tangerine or mandarin orange for each person. Place the sections in the shape of flower petals on each plate. Use a black olive for the center and avocado wedges for the stem and leaves.

Apple tulips can be made by cutting an apple in half and scooping out the core. Lay the halves cut sides down, and cut V's in the tops to resemble tulips. Use avocado wedges for the stems and leaves.

Say something about the advice of Jesus to consider the flowers—and quit worrying!

Use your imagination to turn any fruit salad into a blend of learning and tasting of God's goodness and wisdom. Anything that makes breakfasttime special and that draws thoughts and conversation heavenward will help bring the spirit of peace and reverence to your family.

---

[1] *Century 21 Cookbook*, p. 136.

[2] *Cooking With Natural Foods Cookbook*, p. 17. The Iowa Breakfast Study was reported in the *Breakfast Source Book* (Chicago: Cereal Institute, Inc.).

[3] Adapted from *Country Life Natural Foods Cookbook*.

[4] Adapted from *A Good Cook . . . Ten Talents*, p. 158.

In God's House

"I was glad when they said unto me, Let us go into the house of the Lord" (Ps. 122:1).

*R*everence is a rather vague word to most small children. They need to understand true reverence and to know what is expected of them. To prepare them you might find the following quotation helpful for discussion: "Parents, elevate the standard of Christianity in the minds of your children; help them to weave Jesus into their experience; teach them to have the highest reverence for the house of God and to understand that when they enter the Lord's house, it should be with hearts that are softened and subdued by such thoughts as these: 'God is here; this is His house. I must have pure thoughts and the holiest motives. I must have no pride, envy, jealousy, evil surmising, hatred, or deception in my heart; for I am coming into the presence of the holy God. This is the place where God meets with and blesses His people. The high and holy One who inhabiteth eternity looks upon me, searches my heart, and reads the most secret thoughts and acts of my life.' "—*Child Guidance,* pp. 541, 542.

Mothers with small children find it helpful to prepare diaper bags and purses the night before, to ensure readiness and a spirit of calmness on Sabbath morning. It's just a little thing, but it helps. When my baby was teething, I let him chew on a clean toothbrush once during a meeting. He loved the crunchy bristles against his gums, and it sure did help keep him quiet!

A special day requires special clothes. "All should have a special Sabbath suit, to be worn when attending service in God's house. . . . We are to be neat and trim, though without adornment."—*Ibid.,* p. 531.

Next comes the challenge of having all the children quiet and reverent during church. For the young mother, church can be a trying ordeal. Frequently she'll hear only snatches of the sermon each week. Is it worth it? The blessing is still there for all who attend, and I feel that young mothers and young children especially need God's blessing.

I know of one mother who, every Sabbath morning before leaving the house for church, would pause a moment and offer a word of prayer that the Lord would help all her little ones be quiet and receive a Sabbath day's blessing. I've found this to work even better than any amount of "quiet activities" I may take to entertain the children.

Being a minister's wife, I never have the privilege of sitting with my husband in church and having his help with our children. I certainly sympathize with single parents! To know that I can have the help of God Himself, however, is very reassuring! I cling to the promise of Isaiah 41:10.

The sooner children can get into an attitude of observing everything in church instead of enduring (by reading or playing, et cetera), the better it will be.

Have you ever been tempted to use gum to keep your youngster content and quiet? One day I heard a poem read by a child over the radio that made such an impression on me that I wrote for a copy of it.

Chewing Gum

As I drive along the road
Many things I see.
Yonder are a dozen cows
Gathered 'round the tree.
They have found a refuge;
There they lie and chew their cuds,
Chewing, every one.

Sometimes as I sit in church
Something queer I see
That reminds me of the cows
Gathered 'round the tree.
Men and women, boys and girls,
People everywhere,
Jaws aworking, just like cows—
Funny, I declare!

51

There's no sin in chewing gum,
Guess it isn't wrong,
But there are *some* places
Gum does not belong.
Chew it here, chew it there,
Anyplace you roam;
But when'er you go to church
Leave your gum at home!

Doublemint, Juicy Fruit,
Chew it if you will.
(Now they're even making it
Out of chlorophyll.)
You can find it anyplace
If you'll make the search;
But be sure to leave it home
When you go to church.

Just imagine how we'd look,
In the world to come,
Talking to our blessed Lord,
Mouths afull of gum!

—*Author Unknown*

A nice way to keep your children reverent when they get a little older is to sit in the front where they will not be distracted by others and can see what is going on. Take time to explain the service to them, and then they will be prepared to follow along and take part. If one of your children can read, get a bulletin just for him so he can follow the order of service. He can then be prepared with his money at offering time. He can also find the Scripture reading in advance and put a marker there. When it's time to read it he'll have it ready. Let him be the one to find the song number in the hymnal, and encourage him to sing with you.

One advantage our family has is riding with the preacher to church! He tells the children about an illustration or story he's going to use in his sermon. This helps to awaken their interest, and they tend to listen more attentively.

One Sabbath a little 6-year-old girl came up to my husband after the sermon and talked to him about something he had said. How pleased he was to learn that a little child was listening closely to the sermon! If your child is not too shy, have him listen to the sermon and pick out something to mention to the minister as he shakes his hand at the door. It will certainly brighten your pastor's day, I know!

Never take it for granted that your children understand the sermon. "Parents should explain to their children the words spoken from the pulpit, that they also may understand and have that knowledge which if put into practice brings abundant grace and peace."—*Ibid.*, p. 531.

This doesn't mean you have "roast pastor" for Sabbath dinner! Never should this be a time to criticize anyone or anything pertaining to the church service. I once heard of a great evangelist who said the one thing that drives children out of the church is for them to hear their parents criticize it. We must make our comments positive.

"In listening to the sermon, let parents and children note the text and the scriptures quoted, and as much as possible of the line of thought, to repeat to one another at home. This will go far toward relieving the weariness with which children so often listen to a sermon, and it will cultivate in all a habit of attention and of connected thought."—*Education*, p. 252.

God's House

We come to worship in this place,
To worship God on high.
For we all know that His dear church
Is the apple of His eye.

Sabbath Dinner

"Be kindly affectioned one to another with brotherly love; in honour preferring one another; . . . given to hospitality" (Rom. 12:10-13).

Sabbath dinners have a good reputation in Adventist circles. It was a few months after our refrigerator broke down that I happened to hear a sermon on hospitality versus entertaining. I thought of Sabbath dinners and felt the Holy Spirit speaking to my heart.

I wanted the reputation of being a supercook, keeping a spotless house, and having the best behaved children. I think every woman finds those same basic desires deep within her at one time or another. However, being a minister's wife somehow made me feel that people expected a higher level of perfection in our home than in any other. I found out the hard way that when this expectation is made the rule of thumb or the supreme goal for everyday living, the striving can leave one breathless and a little self-centered. Not to mention the stress it forces on the rest of the family members!

I finally realized that I needed to drop the

burden of entertaining by the world's standards. For instance, I should give up being concerned about how I rated with others and what they would think of me or my house or my children. It was time to take seriously the Bible admonition of 1 Peter 4:9: "Cheerfully share your home with those who need a meal or a place to stay for the night" (T.L.B.).

The day I decided to quit playing society's games and instead keep, with no apologies, a simple and natural but hospitable home, I felt an enormous weight lift from my shoulders. I discovered that hospitality really means loving others and wanting to meet their needs and forgetting about self. I knew that the Bible often admonishes us to be hospitable, but only when I forgot self did hospitality become enjoyable to me.

About this time the children's Sabbath school lesson was on Abraham's and Lot's hospitality and what might have happened to them had they not been hospitable people. The memory verse was Hebrews 13:2: "Be not forgetful to entertain strangers . . . " How often do we do this?

Contrary to popular opinion, Sabbath dinners don't have to be extravaganzas that take so much work to prepare you're exhausted before the blessing! "We should not provide for the Sabbath a more liberal supply or a greater variety of food than for other days. Instead of this the food should be more simple, and less should be eaten. . . . By overeating on the Sabbath, many have done more than they think to dishonor God. . . . Let the meals, though simple, be palatable and attractive. Provide something that will be regarded as a treat, something the family does not have every day."—*Child Guidance*, p. 532.

Not having an overabundance of time or money has forced me to learn that simple meals can still be special. Here are a few ideas that I've found help keep the spirit of Sabbath, and the children love them.

For a tree-of-life salad, use a nice head of broccoli cut in half lengthwise with enough stem to look like the trunk, and cook it just lightly. Serve it on a platter, and put radish halves on top of the "leaves," to represent the fruit. Or smaller individual "trees" for each person can be made with fresh broccoli, and used as a relish with a salad dressing dip. A carrot stick fence could be made around the base of each little tree. Then talk about the tree of life with its twelve different fruits. After your children are in bed on Friday night, take the index to the Spirit of Prophecy writings down and discover all the interesting things Ellen G. White says about the tree of life.

Perhaps if you have a husband who's good at construction or children who enjoy playing with Lincoln Logs, allow them the privilege and fun of making a log cabin out of celery or carrot sticks, chinked with peanut butter. You can then take care of the other dinner preparations. Set the cabin in the center of the table and add little cauliflower or broccoli bushes around the base.

(Just don't get too carried away—you can eat only so many carrot and celery sticks at a time!) You can then spend mealtime talking about the heavenly mansions that the Lord is building for us now. (I have a brother who enjoys raising fish. He hopes one wall of his mansion will be an aquarium. Think of the beauty of it!)

Or you can make candle salads by molding your favorite gelatin dessert in small frozen-juice cans. Unmold them on a bed of lettuce in an upright position for your "candles," and top with mayonnaise or whipping cream "flames." Talk about how God will light our candles (Ps. 18:28), how our spirits are the candles of the Lord (Prov. 20:27), and how the candle of the wicked will be put out (chap. 24:20).

With mashed potatoes you can build a Tower of Babel or Adam's garden. For the garden, spread a thick layer of mashed potatoes on a platter, then make furrows and fill with rows of Brussels sprouts to represent cabbages. Then talk of the blessing of work that God gave to Adam and how a job well done makes a person feel good inside. For the Tower of Babel, talk of how God changed the people's speech back then and how He has the power to change our speech today so that it will be gentle, loving, and patient.

Don't feel that you must do something like this for every Sabbath meal. These little projects are not an end in themselves, but they may help put the sparkle back into the Sabbath for your little ones, and such an approach can help keep the talk of the older people more spiritual. It's a way of putting into practice Deuteronomy 6:7, which tells us to take every opportunity to teach our children the ways of the Lord: "And thou shalt teach them diligently unto thy children, and shalt talk of them when thou sittest in thine house, and when thou walkest by the way, and when thou liest down, and when thou risest up."

Desserts don't have to be rich or heavy, either. Parfait glasses or goblets are pretty when filled with fresh fruit and sprinkled with nuts or coconut. You might want to consider having a Sabbath surprise jar to pass around the table after dinner. This is an opaque container used just for Sabbath. (I use a white plastic gallon jar and decorate it by gluing on bright felt cutouts of a sun, clouds, apple tree, flowers, et cetera.) Put into it a special treat, such as little boxes of carob-coated raisins, bags of salted nuts, or a few cookies wrapped in little squares of bright-colored wrapping paper or tied together with ribbons.

Whatever you use for a Sabbath meal surprise, do not use it during the rest of the week, but keep it special for the Sabbath. This is also the time to use your best dishes, silver, and tablecloths in honor of the unseen Guest.

Often our family enjoys singing the blessing for our Sabbath dinner. We like "Praise God, From Whom All Blessings Flow." It lends an air of thanksgiving to every Sabbath meal and turns the most simple menu into a feast of joy!

Sabbath Afternoon

"The heavens declare the glory of God; and the firmament sheweth his handy-work" (Ps. 19:1).

Dinner is over. Now what? Sabbath school and church services occupy only a few of the Sabbath hours. The rest of the day can be the most sacred and precious of all the Sabbath hours—if we make it so. "Much of this time parents should spend with their children."—*Child Guidance*, p. 532.

I once heard a speaker say that through the years we've gotten the idea that if children would just pedal a little slower, swing a little lower, and play a little quieter, they'd be keeping the Sabbath. But is this God's idea of celebrating the Sabbath?

While rereading the book *Child Guidance*, I discovered that above everything else, parents should take care of their children on the Sabbath. If we allow our children to play inside or even outside on God's holy day, God marks us—the parents—as Sabbathbreakers (page 533).

Here's something that might help. It's a

proven fact that the clothes a person wears affect his behavior. Everyday clothes tell a child, "It's time to play." After church let your children change into special Sabbath afternoon clothes instead of weekday play clothing. This special clothing will remind them that it's still Sabbath.

I've mentioned the book *A Family Guide to Sabbath Nature Activities,* by Eileen E. Lantry. It's a treasure chest of inspirational ideas and things to do on Sabbath afternoons.

But why study nature on Sabbath afternoons? There are many reasons, but I especially like this one found in *Christ's Object Lessons,* page 26: "On the holy rest day, above all other days, we should study the messages that God has written for us in nature. We should study the Saviour's parables where He spoke them, in the fields and groves, under the open sky, among the grass and flowers. *As we come close to the heart of nature, Christ makes His presence real to us, and speaks to our hearts of His peace and love.*" (Italics supplied.)

There is a beautiful alternative to the day of "No, you mustn't do that," "No, that's not a Sabbath toy," "No, we don't do that on Sabbath." The alternative is a day of exciting discoveries about God, a time when we can open our eyes to his wisdom and presence all around us.

Can you hear God's voice in the sighing of the trees? Can you see His power in the majestic mountains? Can you understand His wisdom in the placement of each leaf on every branch so that all may receive proper light? Can you feel the warmth of His love in the sunshine? Can you recognize the effects of the enemy in the great controversy? Sabbath afternoon is an ideal time to study God's "second book."

At first I felt inadequate to teach my children the secrets of nature, but then in the midst of some counsel on Bible study I found good news that can easily apply to nature study: *"As parents become learners with their children, they will find their own growth in grace and in a knowledge of the truth more rapid."—Counsels to Parents and Teachers*, p. 159. (Italics supplied.)

"But my child has no interest in nature," you might object. I found that things like television, worldly music, fairy tales, and fiction make the calm outdoors seem very dull indeed. Remove the unnatural, and with the Lord's help a love for the natural will grow. Once you have felt the presence of God in the great outdoors, you know the sheer joy that comes in discovering a little bit more of Him as the mysteries of nature unfold their secrets before you.

I've found that having a planned nature activity makes it much easier to direct the thoughts of young children. And although I used to always feel fatigued after entertaining guests all afternoon at home, I now always feel refreshed after spending the afternoon outside. So invite your guests, if you happen to have any, to join with you in these nature activities, and your example will be an uplifting influence that will spread like ripples on a pond!

Here are some ideas for nature activities.

Sand pictures. You can create pictures on the ground from the things you find in Mother Nature's storehouse. Divide into pairs to build the pictures. Each couple selects an open place on the ground and then searches for natural objects with which to build a Bible scene. Sticks, flowers, rocks, bark, moss—anything natural—can be used.

May I tell you about one of the prettiest places in the world? It's called Jack's Gulch and is surrounded by the great Rocky Mountains. Aspen groves flutter amid the stately evergreens. Lush grass, sprinkled with wild flowers, hugs a mountain stream, which is fed by a clear, cool spring. Birds cry out as they soar the wide blue sky. Unspoiled by humans, Jack's Gulch remains wild and free.

We were camping there one summer weekend with Grandma and Grandpa. Sabbath afternoon we decided to make sand pictures. Grandma and our older girl, Tracey, paired up. Grandpa chose our boy, Michael, for a partner, and my husband and I took our toddler, Mindy, with us. We all scouted around awhile, gathering supplies. Then each of us chose our spot, and with many cries of "Don't look over here!" we all began to create our pictures. After everyone was finished we went around together to gaze at each one.

Grandpa and Michael had prepared a clever Nativity scene. Oriental-style, from straight pine

63

needles lying flat on the ground. It was very original and nicely framed by firewood.

Lonny, Mindy, and I had done Noah's ark. My husband had deftly constructed an ark out of bark, complete with gangplank. Mindy and I had gathered pinecones, small stones, yellow flowers, blue flowers, and anything else we could find two of, and we had lined them up two by two going into the ark. We completed the picture with moss, grass, and a few twigs to beautify the landscape.

Grandma and Tracey depicted the woman at the well. They found a gopher hole for the well, and with twigs they erected poles above it, complete with little bucket and string. Out of mud and clay, they fashioned a doll-like woman standing and a figure of Jesus sitting. They even fastened leaf clothes on them with long pine needles!

We talked about the sand pictures and enjoyed them for quite a while, not wanting anything to spoil them! We had a memorable time. Once Jesus stooped to write messages in the dust (see John 8:6, 8). And though they were quickly erased, nothing could efface the messages left upon the hearts of those who saw.

Nature sermons. Follow the Saviour's example in using object lessons. While out walking, each one looks for something that will illustrate a spiritual lesson. For example, one Sabbath after a storm we saw a fallen tree weakened by termites. It illustrated the results of sin in the life. Snow reminds us of the pureness of a forgiven heart. A cocoon illustrates death. The caterpillar spins its cocoon and goes to sleep, but awakens a butterfly. Those who die in the Lord also go to sleep and when they awaken at Christ's coming, they too will be changed into new creatures.

A rock can represent Christ. One Sabbath walk, each of us picked up a small rock to carry for the remainder of the hike. We got to know our rocks by feeling them—their peculiar nicks, curves, and bumps. When we got home we put all the rocks into a bag and tried to identify our own rock by touch only. We could because we had become so familiar with it! We talked about how Christ is the "rock" and how we must become familiar with Him so we are not deceived by false christs. Then we sang "The Lord's Our Rock."

Nature matching game. For this game Dad or Mom must first go outside with a paper sack and collect specimens of leaves, bark, flowers, or buds from around the yard. (Buds are very interesting.) Show one of the specimens to the family, then ask them to find the plant, tree, or shrub that it came from. After they have found its source, show them another specimen and have them match it, also. Continue until all the specimens have been matched. This is an excellent way to study and learn trees in all the seasons and to teach that "To every thing there is a season, and a time to every purpose under the heaven" (Eccl. 3:1).

FDTD-5

Days of Creation week. This interesting activity can take seven Sabbaths if you choose. There are so many good ideas for each day's activities and so many spiritual applications to go along with each one that here are just a few "starters" geared for younger children. (Older children can help you study into each day's creation.)

Day one: Blindfold the children and guide them on a short walk. Talk about a world of total darkness. Then discuss light and the rainbow of colors that light can be broken into. Do some demonstrations with a glass prism or magnifying glass. Make a rainbow by spraying your garden hose into the sunlight. "As the bow in the cloud results from the union of sunshine and shower, so the bow above God's throne represents the union of His mercy and His justice."— *Education,* p. 115. Jesus is the light of our world (John 8:12). In heaven the presence of God dispels night and the need for sun in the Holy City (Rev. 21:23, 25). We as Christians are to reflect that light here on earth.

Day two: Discover some things about air. Is it heavy or light? One day we did an experiment that gave us a clue. We taped an empty balloon onto one end of a wooden ruler and a balloon filled with air onto the other end. A string around the very center of the ruler allowed us to hold it up and observe which end was heavier. The weight of air presses down about 14.7 pounds per square inch at sea level. Isn't God wise to have equal air pressure on all sides so that we are not squashed?

Sound travels in waves through the air, enabling us to hear. Air from our lungs makes our vocal cords move, enabling us to speak. Without air we could neither speak nor hear.

Plants use carbon dioxide from air and give off oxygen. People take in oxygen from air and give off carbon dioxide. In God's wisdom He created us to help each other!

Take your little ones outside, lie on your back, and look up at the clouds. Try to copy the shape of one on paper. Talk about the presence of the Holy Spirit and how Jesus likened the Spirit to the wind (see John 3:8).

Day three: Dig a shovelful of dirt and carefully study it. You may be surprised at all you see. Talk about the different kinds of ground in the parable of the sower (Mark 4:3-8, 13-20). Take a magnifying glass outside and study your grass and shrubs through it. For this particular Sabbath, plan a natural meal of the original diet given to man (Gen. 1:29). Save watermelon, squash, or pumpkin seeds, and glue them onto paper in the shape of flowers and trees.

Day four: Get up early to watch the sun rise. Take your breakfast along for a special treat! Or make star maps with little star stickers. Talk about what the sun, moon, and stars were created for (verses 14, 15). Why is Jesus called "the bright morning star" in Revelation 22:16?

Day five: Go for a walk and list all the birds

you see. Put a bird feeder up. Serve a bird's nest salad for dinner. Use a small boiled potato for each person. Grate the potatoes when cold with their peelings still on, using a large grater. Salt and season to taste. Add just enough mayonnaise to hold the shreds together. Form a little nest for each person and put three or four green olives inside for eggs. Sprigs of parsley on either side, or lettuce leaves as a base make this a "treetop" special.

Day six: Study the human body. Make up a matching quiz as to the function of various body organs, after you have studied them. For example: What pumps blood? filters blood? takes and develops pictures? helps maintain body balance? Discuss 1 Corinthians 3:16, 17.

Visit a farm, if you don't live on one, to see the different animals and the care given them. Ask if you could milk a cow or goat or gather some eggs. A museum might work for some occasions.

Day seven: Talk about how Jesus did good on the Sabbath. He always thought of others. Pick a missionary project for the whole family to get involved in, and spend a portion of the afternoon doing it. Our family saves *Our Little Friend, Primary Treasure, Signs,* and *Liberty* magazines. We always pray over them first and then take them to a special Laundromat downtown that we picked out. The magazines are always gone each time we return. We were really thrilled the first time a lady left her washer to pick up a magazine we had just left. As we drove away we could see her reading it. It's a small thing, but it's something we can do every week. Even our shyest child can take part, planting seeds of truth that we pray will not return void unto the Lord.

Some excellent aids for your days-of-Creation activities (for preschool- through grade-school-age children) are the Childcraft books *The Green Kingdom, World and Space,* and *About Me,* available at most public or school libraries. They contain beautiful pictures and are easy to understand.

Look and see. In advance of this nature walk, draw for the children an observation sheet of things that they would be likely to see on the walk. I use 3 x 5 index cards and then put each child's card in a plastic Baggie along with as many gold star stickers as there are items on the list. When the children see one of the objects pictured on their list, they may stick a star beside it. Pictures work best for small children. On the observation sheets for the older children, write or type the list of objects to be seen. The sheets can be simple for the younger children, with objects such as a cat, dog, flower, and bird; or harder for older children, by listing certain species of birds, names of trees, certain flowers, or rocks. We've done this activity quite often, especially when we have guests with children, and we always enjoy the challenge of finding everything on the list!

Nature treasure hunt. This activity is similar to the previous one, only you bring back the nature items that are required. Give each child a bag and a list such as this one: (1) pinecone, (2) manzanita leaf, (3) evergreen needle, (4) feather, (5) seed, (6) leaf of a certain color, (7) red stone, (8) cattail, (9) piece of bark, (10) quartz rock, (11) moss, (12) flower, (13) mushroom, (14) insect, dead or alive, and (15) a very crooked twig.

Nature treasure hike. On this hike all participants keep their eyes and ears open for a "nature treasure" that the Lord might send. Usually on every hike we see something special. It may be a deer or a swarm of ladybugs. One Sabbath after our hike was over, we were back at the lake's edge where we had started from. It was beginning to get dark, and the shadows were flickering on the marsh grass. Suddenly the frogs began to sing. It was high-fidelity stereo! And just a few inches in front of us was a little frog singing his heart out. We watched him for at least ten minutes as he pushed his bulgy throat sack out, out, out, and croaked, croaked, croaked! Our youngest child looked at me happily and said, "Mama, this is the Sabbath nature treasure God gave us today!" And I agreed.

Diamond trail. Prepare ten or so orange diamond-shaped pieces of paper. On each one put a Bible text pertaining to some nature item on the "trail," and on the other side give directions to the next "diamond." For example, I'll share what our family did one Sabbath.

It was going to be a beautiful, sunny summer day, I could tell. The sunrise was spectacular, as

Colorado sunrises usually are, and the children hadn't awakened yet. I slipped out of the house with the ten diamonds I had just made and roamed about the property surrounding our country home, hiding them like Easter eggs.

We had invited some new members home for Sabbath dinner, and afterward we asked them if they would like to go on a "diamond hunt" with us. They agreed, so we were off. The two older girls took Bibles, because they could read. If I remember right, it went something like this. "No. 1—Look under a rock that borders the flower bed." When they found the rock that the diamond was under, they also found the ants' home and tunnels filled with big ant eggs. One of the girls looked up Proverbs 6:6, which advises us to study the ants and be wise.

The next clue was "Look in the rosebush for No. 2." The children carefully reached in to get the diamond; and John 19:2, which tells of Jesus' crown of thorns, took on more meaning.

On the back of that diamond was the clue "Look in the rafters of the shed for No. 3." They found that diamond hidden near a bird's nest on which sat the mother bird. The verse was Psalm 91:4: "He shall cover thee with his feathers, and under his wings shalt thou trust."

The back of that diamond read: "Go to the apple tree for No. 4." And away everyone dashed. The verse was Psalm 17:8: "Keep me as the apple of your eye" (N.I.V.).

Then they ran to the old antique wagon out

71

front, and hidden in one of the large wooden wheels was diamond No. 5. The verse was Jeremiah 18:3, and we explained how a potter's wheel works.

On the back of that card were directions to the neighbor's lilac hedge, covered with thick purple flower clusters. The verse for No. 6 was Song of Solomon 3:9, 10, which describes in detail the private chariot King Solomon made for himself.

The next clue was "Search in the tall grass past the swings for No. 7." It took all of the children a while to find that diamond hidden in the grass. The verse was Isaiah 40:8: "The grass withereth, the flower fadeth; but the word of our God shall stand for ever."

It was off to the "locust tree on the north side of the yard" for No. 8. The text was Matthew 3:4, and we discussed the locusts and honey that John the Baptist ate.

The next clue led us to the little "willow tree east of the house" for No. 9, and the verse was Ezekiel 17:5, which speaks of a willow tree.

The last clue was "Follow the road west for one-quarter mile to the big pond for No. 10." The text was John 4:13, 14, which tells of the water of life and how it differs from ordinary drinking water.

The older children loved the challenge of finding the diamonds, and we were able to talk about some interesting spiritual things as we read the verses.

Our baby enjoyed riding on Daddy's shoulders and being out in the sunshine of God's great world. This is a good way to use your own yard to study nature. Just use a concordance to discover what the Bible has to say about the many things that surround you.

Progressive hike. A progressive hike is always interesting to boys and girls. On it you stop periodically for a preplanned activity. One Sabbath we had two families over to our house, which swelled the number of children (mostly preschool age) to eight. After dinner we drove to a beautiful wooded trail, three and a half miles long, that had resting benches every so often along the way. We told the children that at every park bench we would have a special activity to do. The children really enjoyed hurrying from bench to bench!

Bench #1: Each child received ten small stones. I then asked ten Bible questions. Each time a child knew an answer to a question, he said nothing but quietly dropped a stone to the ground. The object was to be perfectly honest with himself regardless of what others around him were doing.

Bench #2: Sand pictures. We divided up and scurried around, eyes alert for nature's valuables. Minds were whirling as we planned scenes that the others could guess. We got a little idea of the excitement Jesus must have felt as He knelt in the dirt to make Adam!

Bench #3: An activity sheet. I used *My Sabbath Fun Book*, by Cecilia M. Watson (available at your ABC). The little ones did a Bible dot-to-dot, while the older ones worked on a crossword puzzle. The sounds of the surrounding woods made delightful background music.

Bench #4: Storytime. Daddy read an exciting mission story while everyone paused to rest. Then we had prayer.

Flower collecting. Children love to pick flowers. We should teach them early to be sensitive nature lovers. If we allow them to pick flowers just to throw away, they learn carelessness. On your walk, repeat often the names of any wildflowers you have picked. Then ask your children to name the same ones they see growing along the way.

Once home, you may want to press the flowers carefully between paper towels and then between books. The children will love to see them after several days. One Sabbath our older daughter made a special bookmark and put some of her pressed flowers on it, along with a nice Bible verse. She then covered it with clear contact paper. She gave it to a friend that afternoon at her baptism.

Flowers may also be dried by putting them upside down on clean, dry sand in a small box. Carefully cover the flowers with more sand. Keep them undisturbed for two or three weeks.

If you would have your Sabbath afternoon nature activity be a total success, I would suggest one more thing. Before you start, pause for a moment of prayer, asking the Holy Spirit to be

with you and direct your thoughts to an under-
standing of what God would have you to learn on
this Sabbath. Then enjoy every golden moment
the afternoon affords!

"Earth's crammed with heaven,
    And every common bush afire with God;
        But only he who sees
            Takes off his shoes."
                —Elizabeth Barrett Browning

Rainy-Day Sabbaths

"From the rising of the sun unto the going down of the same the Lord's name is to be praised" (Ps. 113:3).

Some Sabbaths you'll have to spend indoors, which provides an ideal time to teach your youngsters that "it is lawful to do well on the sabbath" (Matt. 12:12) and that happiness comes from helping others. In thinking of others, let's not forget that God loves the elderly! In fact, He tells us to "rise in the presence of grey hairs, give honour to the aged, and fear your God" (Lev. 19:32, N.E.B.).

Invite three of your child's friends over and plan a program to put on at a nursing home. Choose several songs to sing. Pick someone to read a scripture and someone to say a prayer. A simple and short program, but a real blessing to everyone.

Children also like to decorate love baskets and deliver them to the elderly or shut-in members of the church. We asked a friend of ours to save her green plastic strawberry boxes for us. Our children by this time were ages 10, 7, and nearly 4. They all enjoyed weaving three rows of different colored ribbon through the baskets and putting bright pipe cleaner handles on the tops. They were then ready to line the baskets with napkins and fill them with a small loaf of tasty bread or with homemade cookies. Then we delivered the baskets to some elderly friends.

At this age children also love to cut and paste. Save nature calendar pictures to be cut up and put into a scrapbook for a lonely hospital patient. Use brightly colored construction paper on which to glue the pictures. I like to frame the cutout pictures with rickrack, cut and glued to the edges of the pictures. Different sizes and colors of rickrack around the pictures make a page very attractive. I either write or type special verses that match the theme of the pictures on each page. Bind five or six pages together with yarn, and you have a delightful little scrapbook to share.

In the fall our children have enjoyed hunting and saving brightly colored leaves to put between two pieces of clear contact paper. They then trim around the shape of the leaf, making a pretty bookmark. We have also added a short Bible verse typed on colored construction paper. When we go to a nursing home to sing, the children enjoy passing out these bookmarks to everyone.

If you know of a blind person or elderly person who would enjoy being read to, ask your older child to read to him. Help your child read with clarity and expression. Both child and listener will be blessed.

77

Children love Bible charades (acting out Bible stories). The family could invite an elderly person home for dinner, and then the guest can be the "audience." Such activities can brighten an otherwise lonely day for the older folk, and delight your children, too.

Perhaps you have a teenager who enjoys driving the family car. What an ideal time to take a shut-in for a scenic ride in the country, if the weather's not too bad.

Another thing to do on rainy Sabbaths is to make a spiritual scrapbook of answers to prayer. Keep it up-to-date with pictures (drawn or taken) and all the details of every answer to prayer. Then get it out and relive the incidents together on a Sabbath afternoon. Don't forget lost toys that were found, help on school tests, and everyday answers to prayer. Children enjoy retelling the stories, and it strengthens faith!

Once Tracey needed shoes for school. At that time our budget didn't include even 10 cents for shoes, so during worship I suggested that we ask God for a pair of shoes for Tracey. About one week later her teacher gave her a box all wrapped and said someone had given it to her to give to Tracey. Inside was a beautiful new pair of shoes just her size!

Or you can work on Adventist Youth Honors that pertain to nature. For instance, there's an Honor for stars. Make star constellations by punching holes with an ice pick through the sides of a large box. Apple or orange boxes work great. Then show the pattern with a strong light bulb or flashlight in the box. Of course, darken the room for effect. Study the constellations with your children on rainy Sabbaths, then on a clear, starry night try to locate the constellations in the sky. Remind your children that God "telleth the number of the stars, he calleth them all by their names" (Ps. 147:4). Help them anticipate the thrilling space trip every child of God can take someday! Acquaint them with the open space in Orion through which the New Jerusalem will descend (*Early Writings*, p. 41).

Flowers you have dried on previous occasions can be taped into a scrapbook and categorized, or they can be preserved in wax. Paraffin comes in four blocks to a box. Use one teaspoon of mineral oil for each block of wax. Heat until melted and dip the dried flowers in and out of the wax.

One thing our family enjoys (even our toddler) is to form Bible objects out of modeling clay. We each sit at the table with a plastic place mat and ball of clay apiece. When a person has finished creating something, he says so, and then the others try to guess what it is. Some things like Moses' staff, Abel's altar, and Jacob's well are easy to make.

Here's a fun game for little people just learning phonics. If you have a Scrabble game, put the letter tiles in a jar. Whichever letter of the alphabet you draw out, think of a Bible word that begins with the same letter. For example, *A* could stand for Adam, *B* could be for Bible, *C* could be for Canaan. Go around the circle until all the alphabet tiles are used up.

One rainy Sabbath afternoon the phone rang while our family was watching a nature film-strip.* My husband answered it and then told us that some people were on their way over to see us. Michael perked up and exlaimed curiously, "I wonder what these people will be like!" They turned out to be a lovely couple with three young children. The father was thinking of going back to school to prepare for the ministry.

"We just wanted to see what a minister's family is like," the father said as they were leaving several hours later. I was glad that while they visited with us, all six children were busy and happy doing the following nature activity. Not once did they want to go to the children's rooms and play, and as a parent I was thankful for ideas that we could put into practice at a moment's notice.

First, we let the children collect different kinds of leaves from our yard. They had to use an umbrella while they were outside. They placed the leaves under plain white paper on the table and then colored back and forth over them, making attractive leaf designs. We then had a guessing game to identify the kinds of leaves the children had collected. When the children tired of that, we let them glue the leaves to construction paper in the shape of animals or nature scenes—big leaves for bodies, long slender leaves for legs, et cetera.

Here's another activity for a rainy Sabbath. Make a mural. You can purchase very inexpensively large rolls of unused paper ends from your local newspaper office. This paper works great for a mural, and a lot of other things, too! Use either crayons or some oil pastels. (These are nontoxic oil colors in stick form that you can buy at a variety-type store. They are brighter and prettier than regular crayons.) Choose a Bible character whose life you wish to depict. For instance, Daniel, Joseph, Miriam, or Jesus. Assign each family member a space of the paper for a certain event or time period in that person's life. Tape your finished paper across a wall.

One Sabbath our two younger children had colds, so we stayed home from church. We always have our own Sabbath school whenever we have to miss regular services, so we got ready to do their lesson of Noah and the Flood. I put the back of a chair up against the front of our couch and threw a large blanket over it and the back of the couch, which made the "ark." The children brought all their stuffed animals and stored them inside. I cut a large rainbow out of a roll of paper and taped it to our sliding glass doors. Each of us colored a ribbon strip of the rainbow, which looked very pretty with the sun shining through it.

"I went into Noah's ark" is another animal game. Everyone sits in the living room while one person goes out. That person then comes in and acts like a certain animal that entered Noah's ark. The rest of the family try to guess what animal he is.

Don't forget the joy of a sing-along. Gather around the piano if you have one, or get out the instruments (homemade ones if need be or just small bells), and sing, sing, sing!

"As the sun goes down, let the voice of prayer and the hymn of praise mark the close of the sacred hours, and invite God's presence through the cares of the week of labor.

"Thus parents can make the Sabbath, as it should be, the most joyful day of the week. They can lead their children to regard it as a delight, the day of days, the holy of the Lord, honorable."—*Child Guidance*, pp. 536, 537.

---

* Most public libraries have National Geographic and other nature filmstrips to check out.

Afterglow

Sabbath is over for another week. Life's many duties must be picked up again and dealt with faithfully. A twinge of sadness settles over me at the setting of the sun. Yet God promises with each Sabbath an afterglow of blessings that warm and color each day of life.

One of these blessings is the promise of sanctification. God promised the children of Israel that Sabbathkeeping was a sign of their sanctification. "Moreover also I gave them my sabbaths, to be a sign between me and them, that they might know that I am the Lord that sanctify them" (Eze. 20:12). My Funk and Wagnalls *Standard College Dictionary* defines *sanctify* as "to set apart as holy or for holy purposes; consecrated." In Leviticus 19:2 we read, "Ye shall be holy: for I the Lord your God am holy." Paul tells us that these promises to ancient Israel are just as valid for spiritual Israel today (see Rom. 9:6-8). I can be a part of spiritual Israel, for Galatians 3:9, 29 says, "So then they which be of faith are blessed with faithful Abraham."

"And if ye be Christ's, then ye are Abraham's seed, and heirs according to the promise."

As I prepare nutritious meals, read stories to the children, and encourage my husband I feel humbly honored that I am set apart for holy use. "Holiness is wholeness for God; it is the entire surrender of heart and life to the indwelling of the principles of heaven."—*The Desire of Ages*, p. 556.

On some days it's a real struggle to do right, and sometimes I fail. The goals God has for me seem too high, and I look at myself and get discouraged. Have you ever felt that way? Then Jesus says, "Come unto me, all ye that labour and are heavy laden, and I will give you rest" (Matt. 11:28). Jesus' words apply to our attempts at salvation by our own works. "For he spake in a certain place of the seventh day on this wise, And God did rest on the seventh day from all his works. . . . There remaineth therefore a rest to the people of God. For he that is entered into his rest, he also hath ceased from his own works, as God did from his. Let us labour therefore to enter into that rest, lest any man fall after the same example of unbelief" (Heb. 4:4-11).

Jesus wants us to remember that it is He who sanctifies us and not we ourselves. Sabbath is a weekly reminder that my strength comes in surrending and that my rest is in the righteousness of Christ. Furthermore, I can trust Him to finish what He has started in my life. Wonderful Jesus!

Another blessing is that I enjoy better health each week from stopping every seventh day for spiritual refreshment. "Thou shalt not do any work," the commandment says. This includes housework. Anything that I can do on any other day should not rob time on Sabbath. Sometimes it's hard to leave some things undone until after Sabbath. But I am beginning to see why God made certain restrictions for the Sabbath day. He is concerned about our physical health. "Beloved, I wish above all things that thou mayest prosper and be in health, even as thy soul prospereth" (3 John 2).

God gives us fifty-two Sabbaths, or seven and a half weeks, of vacation time a year! Time during which we are to do no work. Time that allows us to be recharged physically, mentally, and spiritually.

Another blessing I've discovered is a feeling of security in an uncertain world. Remember the words of Isaiah 58:13, 14? God tells us that if we honor the Sabbath by putting self aside and if we make it a delight, then we will find our joy in the Lord. It is true! We become His chosen, and He becomes our Beloved. We are wed in spiritual oneness, and "I am persuaded, that neither death, nor life, nor angels, nor principalities, nor powers, nor things present, nor things to come, nor height, nor depth, nor any other creature, shall be able to separate us from the love of God, which is in Christ Jesus our Lord" (Rom. 8:38, 39).

I also thank God for the Sabbath blessings that bind together and save families. Child rearing can be a pretty scary business these days. I have found that if the Sabbath is rightly observed, it offers a built-in period of time for busy parents to bind the hearts of their children to them and to their Creator. It provides for the Elijah message to take effect in our homes. "And he shall turn the heart of the fathers to the children, and the heart of the children to their fathers, lest I come and smite the earth with a curse" (Mal. 4:6).

Sad to say, my children have often had to tag along behind me while I work, just to talk to me. I seem to be always busy. But on Sabbath there's no excuse! I can take time to listen to my children with both ears open. The Sabbath is God's safeguard against generation gaps, and He will reward faithful parents. "Blessed is the man that feareth the Lord, that delighteth greatly in his commandments. His seed shall be mighty upon the earth: the generation of the upright shall be blessed" (Ps. 112:1, 2).

Another grand and prophetic promise is "And they that shall be of thee shall build the old waste places: thou shalt raise up the foundations of many generations; and thou shalt be called, The repairer of the breach, The restorer of paths to dwell in" (Isa. 58:12).

A breach was made in the law of God when mankind attempted to change the Sabbath to Sunday. But this breach is to be repaired! If we parents keep the Sabbath in all holiness, we will "raise up the foundations of many generations," and our children will "build the old waste places" and help us restore the paths to heaven so that many may walk therein and be saved. If our children are doing this they won't be in the world drinking from the devil's polluted fountains. What wonderful promises for our precious children! What awesome responsibility for parents!

And does the Sabbath offer any glimmer of hope to marriages? In this day and age when nearly half of all American marriages end in divorce, I feel that the Sabbath can be a key factor in the successful and happy union of husbands and wives. As couples see the beautiful roles of Christ and His bride portrayed in Ephesians 5:21-33 they can better understand their relationship to each other. When wives see Christ as head of the church, they will honor and respect their husbands more as the head of their homes. And as husbands fall in love with their Saviour, who, as their example, gave His life for His bride, they will love and cherish their wives with Christian faithfulness.

The Sabbath provides one whole day each week when Dad's thoughts are not wrapped up in his success or failure in the rat race of life. One day when Mom's hands can rest from ceaseless labor. One day when they can walk arm in arm on a nature walk among the trees, smile at each other in the sunshine, pick and give a flower that says, "I love you," and feel the closeness and security of a united family.

The devil has had much time to work his will in our world. In the very beginning God admonished Adam and Eve to stay together. They were to work together, play together, worship together, learn together. When they became separated Satan tempted Eve to sin, and Satan has been busy separating families ever since. First, he took the father away from home to work. Next, he took the children away from home to be taught. Now mothers leave home and work to make ends meet or to feel fulfilled. There's not much left of God's original plan for the home, but He has called a halt when it comes to the Sabbath. It remains the day of all days when we are most able to live the life of Eden.

"It was God's plan for the members of the family to be associated in work and study, in worship and recreation, the father as priest of his household, and both father and mother as teachers and companions of their children. But the results of sin, having changed the conditions of life, to a great degree prevent this association. Often the father hardly sees the faces of his children throughout the week. He is almost wholly deprived of opportunity for companionship or instruction. But God's love has set a limit to the demands of toil. Over the Sabbath He places His merciful hand. In His own day He preserves for the family opportunity for communion with Him, with nature, and with one another."—*Education*, pp. 250, 251.

I have discovered many more blessings that come with the Sabbath! We are promised in Isaiah 58:14 that He will cause us "to ride upon the high places of the earth" (K.J.V.). "I saw that we sensed and realized but little of the importance of the Sabbath, to what we yet should realize and know of its importance and glory. I saw we knew not what it was yet to ride upon the high places of the earth and to be fed with the heritage of Jacob. But when the refreshing and latter rain shall come from the presence of the Lord and the glory of His power, we shall know what it is to be fed with the heritage of Jacob and ride upon the high places of the earth. Then shall we see the Sabbath more in its importance and glory.

"But we shall not see it in all its glory and importance until the covenant of peace is made with us at the voice of God, and the pearly gates of the New Jerusalem are thrown open and swing back on their glittering hinges, and the glad and joyful voice of the lovely Jesus is heard richer than any music that ever fell on mortal ear bidding us enter."—*Selected Messages*, book 3, p. 388.

Of course, times will come occasionally when the devil makes everything go wrong and it's a struggle to keep priorities straight. No matter how well you plan there will be times when you feel too tired to lead out in a Sabbath afternoon activity, and times when the cooperation of the family might not be very visible. Perhaps some members of your family won't want to change their idea of a rest day—sleeping all afternoon!

Don't become discouraged! Remember Galatians 6:9: "And let us not be weary in well doing: for in due season we shall reap, if we faint not." And the most exciting promise of all is Revelation 22:14: "Blessed are they that do his commandments, that they may have right to the tree of life, and may enter in through the gates into the city."

No longer do I think of Sabbath as a dilemma, for it has become the doorway to a wonderful relationship with Jesus Christ my Lord. It provides destiny and purpose in living for me and precious promises for my family. I hope and pray that every Sabbath will be a delight for you and your family until the Lord comes—and then every Sabbath will be heavenly!

> There's a promise in the rainbow
> As it stretches through the sky.
> There are blessings in the Sabbath,
> And you'll find them if you try!